YOUR KNOWLEDGE HAS

- We will publish your bachelor's and master's thesis, essays and papers

- Your own eBook and book - sold worldwide in all relevant shops

- Earn money with each sale

Upload your text at www.GRIN.com
and publish for free

Manfred Fettinger

Intrusion Detection in Wireless Ad Hoc Networks

Comparison of Different Approaches

GRIN Publishing

Bibliographic information published by the German National Library:

The German National Library lists this publication in the National Bibliography;
detailed bibliographic data are available on the Internet at http://dnb.dnb.de .

Imprint:

Copyright © 2009 GRIN Verlag GmbH
Print and binding: Books on Demand GmbH, Norderstedt Germany
ISBN: 978-3-640-37665-0

This book at GRIN:

http://www.grin.com/en/e-book/131753/intrusion-detection-in-wireless-ad-hoc-
networks

GRIN - Your knowledge has value

Since its foundation in 1998, GRIN has specialized in publishing academic texts by students, college teachers and other academics as e-book and printed book. The website www.grin.com is an ideal platform for presenting term papers, final papers, scientific essays, dissertations and specialist books.

Visit us on the internet:

http://www.grin.com/

http://www.facebook.com/grincom

http://www.twiller.com/grln_com

Fachhochschule Technikum Wien

Bachelor Thesis

Intrusion Detection in Wireless Ad Hoc Networks - Comparison of Different Approaches

Written by Manfred Fettinger

Vienna, 10.06.2009

Kurzfassung

Kabellose ad-hoc Netzwerke sind Netzwerke, die ohne jegliche Infrastruktur auskommen. Dadurch sind diese sehr gefährdet angegriffen zu werden. Ein Angreifer hat nicht wie in einem verkabelten Netzwerk Firewalls oder Gateways zu passieren, daher wurden verschiedenste Intrusion Detection Systeme entwickelt. Diese Arbeit präsentiert verschiedene Intrusion Detection Architekturen, erklärt ihre Arbeitsweise und vergleicht diese. Weiters wird gezeigt, wie die Spieltheorie genutzt werden kann, um die Effizienz von Intrusion Detection zu steigern.

Abstract

Wireless ad-hoc networks are networks without any infrastructure. Due to this fact they are very vulnerable to attacks. Adversaries do not have to pass different barriers like gateways or firewalls like in wired networks. Therefore different architectures for intrusion detection were developed. The contribution of this paper is to present different intrusion detection architectures, explains their behaviour and compare them. Furthermore it is shown how game theory can be used to improve performance of intrusion detection.

Keywords: Intrusion Detection, Wireless Ad-Hoc Networks, MANET, Architecture

Acknowledgements

Thanks to Cristina Comaniciu and Hong Man for using figures out of [7], Udo Pooch and Bo Sun for giving permission to use figures from [12]. Also Herve Debar for giving permission to use figures out of [3]. Furthermore to Dipl.-Ing. Dr. Karl Göschka for supporting me during my bachelor thesis.

Table of Contents

1 Introduction

Wireless ad-hoc networks are networks without any infrastructure and have a dynamic topology. Nodes have only limited physical security and are limited in resources. In principle every node in this network has equal rights, every node can independently join or leave the network. Due to the lack of any infrastructure the nodes have to organize the network themselves. Nodes can communicate directly within their transmission range if the target node is out of reach, other nodes have to act as routers. That means every node in a wireless ad-hoc network functions also as a router and the success of communication depends on other nodes' cooperation [13]. These networks are used where an infrastructure is not available, e.g. on battlefields, business associates sharing information in meetings, attendees using laptops to participate in interactive conferences, emergency disaster relief and personal area [13].

A wireless ad-hoc network is very vulnerable to attacks because an adversary has not to pass different barriers like firewalls or gateways, like it is in infrastructure based environments [16]. Intrusion detection systems (IDS) can help finding out if a network is under attack and initiate counteractive measures. An IDS can be described as the second wall of defence whereas intrusion prevention is meant as the first wall of defence [15]. In a infrastructure based network, traffic monitoring is normally done at traffic concentration points like switches, routers and gateways. Due to the lack of infrastructure this approach is not suitable for wireless networks. Therefore most approaches focus on using a detection engine on each node of the wireless network.

A distinction of IDS, based of the audit data used, can be made between network-based and host-based IDS [15]. A network based IDS runs at the gateway of a network and there it captures and examines all passing network packets. The host-based IDS, which is installed on every node, relies on operating system audit data. It monitors and analyzes all events generated by programs and users of the host.

Techniques of intrusion detection can be split into misuse and anomaly detection systems. Misuse detection systems use patterns of well-known attacks to match and identify intrusions [15]. For example the number of login attempts within one minute could be such a pattern. The accurate and efficient detection of attacks is the advantage of this type, on the other hand misuse detection lacks of the ability to detect new invented attacks [15]. The problem is that a database where the patterns are saved has to be updated frequently and this maintenance is a lot of work and is mostly behind new invented attacks. Anomaly detection systems observe activities that deviate significantly from established normal usage profiles as anomalies e.g. the average frequencies of system commands [15]. [9] makes also a further distinction to specification-based detection systems, there a set of constraints describe the correct operation of a program or protocol. The execution is monitored with respect to the defined constraints. There are a lot of different architectures e.g. [16], [5], [4], [12] available. In this paper these four different types are presented and discussed.

The rest of the paper is organized as follows. Section 2 gives an overview of security attacks on different layers of the Internet protocol. In sections 3 to 6 above mentioned different architectures of IDS are presented. In section 7 it is explained how game theory can help to increase performance in ID. Section 8 compares all introduced architectures and points out most important differences. Last section 9 closes this work with a conclusion.

2 Overview of Security attacks

This section describes most relevant security attacks, classifies them and gives a good overview of attacks on different layers. Afterwards attacks on each layer of the Internet model are explained. Most information is taken from [13].

2.1 Classification of attacks

First a difference is made between active and passive attacks. In a passive attack, the adversary obtains data which is exchanged in the network without disrupting the operation of communications nor destroying or modifying any data. Whereas an active attack is classified through an interruption, modification or fabrication of communication data. Examples of passive attacks are eavesdropping, traffic analysis and traffic monitoring [13]. Active attacks are jamming, impersonating, modification, denial of service (DoS) and message replay [13]. The whole difference of them is that a concerned person or node does not take any notice of a passive attack whereas an active attack can and in some cases should be noticed by the target.

Second, external and internal attacks are differentiated. An external attack occurs when a node outside of the networks´ domain attacks a node inside the network. In contrast an internal attack describes an attack where a node, which is part of the network, places an attack. An internal attack is more dangerous than an external one due to the knowledge of valuable and secret information and privileged access rights. As example, the internal attacker may know important IP addresses and the security policy of the target area.

The next classification is done between stealthy and non-stealthy attacks. If an attacker tries to hide his action from an individual or an intrusion detection system, then we speak about a stealthy attack. On the other hand a non-stealthy attack is an attack which cannot be made stealthy like DoS. It is also clear that the aim of some attacks is to be non-stealthy, otherwise they would be useless.

Furthermore a difference between cryptography and non-cryptography related attacks is done. Cryptographic attacks [13] are classified into

- Pseudorandom number attacks

    o timestamp, initialization vector

- Digital signature attacks

    o RSA signature, ElGamal signature, digital signature standard

- Hash collision attacks

    o SHA-0, MD4, MD5, HAVAL-128, RIPEMD

At least attacks on different layers of the internet model are distinguished. Table 1 shows different attacks which are possible on each layer, whereas some attacks can be used on multiple layers [13].

Layer	Attacks
Application layer	Repudiation, data corruption
Transport layer	Session hijacking, SYN flooding
Network layer	Wormhole, blackhole, Byzantine, flooding, resource consumption, location disclosure attacks
Data link layer	Traffic analysis, monitoring, disruption MAC (802.11), WEP weakness
Physical layer	Jamming, interceptions, eavesdropping
Multi-layer attacks	DoS, impersonation, replay, man-in-the-middle

Table 1: Attacks on different layers of the Internet Model

The next section will explain each attack on the concerning layer. Fist attacks on the physical layer are explained.

2.2 Physical layer attacks

As wireless communication is broadcast by nature common radio signals are very easy to jam or intercept. An adversary can easily overhear or disrupt a service of a wireless network physically [13]. Next sections present eavesdropping and jamming as attacks on the physical layer.

2.2.1 Eavesdropping

The aim of an eavesdropping attack is to read and intercept messages by unintended receivers. Therefore signals or messages can be overheard also fake messages can be injected [13]. Those attacks fall in the category of passive attacks due to the fact the sender and receiver of a message take no notice if messages are overheard. Fake messages are due to fabrication of new messages assigned to the category of active attacks. Hence an eavesdropping attack can be both, active or passive, depending on the fulfilment.

2.2.2 Interference and jamming

Through interference and jamming, radio signals can be disrupted. In the case of a powerful transmitter, signals can be overwhelmed and therefore get disrupted by an attacker [13]. The consequences are corruption or lost of messages. Interference and jamming are assigned to the part of active attacks. The next section is dedicated to the link layer.

2.3 Link layer attacks

Wireless ad-hoc networks are open multipoint peer-to-peer networks. Connectivity among neighbours is maintained by the link layer protocol while the network layer protocol extends the connectivity to all other nodes in the network. Therefore attackers may target the link

3

layer protocol by disrupting the cooperation of the two layers protocols [13]. As examples a backoff mechanism and the weakness of 802.11 WEP[1] are introduced in the next sections.

2.3.1 Disruption on MAC[2] DCF[3] and backoff mechanism

MAC protocols currently assume cooperative behaviour of all nodes. If malicious nodes do not follow the protocol specifications they can interrupt connection-based or reservation-based MAC protocols [13]. Thus it is possible that an attacker exploits its binary exponential backoff scheme to deny access to the wireless channel from its neighbours [14].

2.3.2 Weakness of 802.11 WEP

WEP introduced by IEEE 802.11 provides WLAN system a modest level of privacy by encrypting radio signals [13]. Although it is common that WEP is broken and replaced by AES[4] it is still in use. The problem of WEP is that the initialization vector (IV) consists only of 3 bytes. Therefore the probability that the same IV is chosen a second time is very high and is reached after approximately 5.000 network packets sent. This is equivalent to 7 megabytes of data. Hence the password is not changed the attacker has two ciphered packets which were encrypted with the same key. If the attacker knows the plaintext of one of them (may he has forced a message) he can easily decrypt the other [6]. The next higher layer of the Internet Model is the network layer which is presented next.

2.4 Network layer attacks

As mentioned in section 2.3 the network layer extends connectivity from neighbouring nodes to all other nodes of a network [13]. For correct communication over multi-hop links it is necessary that every node cooperates in this task. If a malicious node doesn't cooperate it can lead to a corruption of the routing protocol. There are a lot of different attacks possible:

- Attacks at the routing discovery phase

- Routing table overflow attack

- Routing cache poisoning attack

- Attacks at the routing maintenance phase

- Attacks at data forwarding phase

- Attacks on particular routing protocols

- Others (Wormhole-, Blackhole-, Byzantine attack, ...)

---

[1] Wired Equivalent Privacy

[2] Medium Access Control

[3] Distributed Coordination Function

[4] Advanced Encryption Standard

4

A detailed description of each of them can be found in [13]. Attacks which can occur on the transport layer are now explained in the next section.

2.5 Transport layer attacks

The main task of the transport layer is to set up an end-to-end connection and to guarantee a reliable delivery of packets over it, which includes flow control, congestion control and the clearing of the connection [13]. Compared with wired networks, wireless ad-hoc networks have a higher channel error rate. Following syn flooding and session hijacking are explained.

2.5.1 Syn flooding attack

Syn flooding is an attack which can be categorized under DoS attacks. For a better understanding of this attack it is necessary to know about the three-way-handshake.

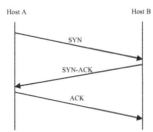

Fig. 1: Three way handshake protocol

Figure 2 shows the flow of a three-way-handshake (3WHS). This protocol is used by TCP whenever a connection is established or teared down. First host A sends a SYN message to host B then host B acknowledge this message by a SYN-ACK message. Finally host A sends an acknowledge message ACK back to host B. Now both hosts can begin to communicate. When a connection is teared down the SYN message is replaced by a FIN message.

The syn flooding attack does nothing other than create a huge number of half opened TCP connections but never completes the handshake. That means that a malicious node sends a SYN request to a target node but never sends the ACK message back. Therefore the target node must maintain all requests until a buffer overflow occurs. To avoid those attacks a node could let the half opened connections expire, however the malicious node can continue sending SYN packets faster than the expiration happens.

2.5.2 Session hijacking

This attack uses the fact that most communications are protected at session setup but not thereafter. The attacker spoofs the victim's IP address, determines the correct sequence number that is expected by the target and performs a DoS attack on the victim. Furthermore the attacker impersonates the victim and continues the session with the target [13]. The next section completes the presentation of attacks on layers of the Internet Model. This last layer is the application layer.

2.6 Application layer attacks

The application layer supports many protocols like http, SMTP, TELNET and FTP. Hence there are many targets for an attacker. Due to the fact that a user works mostly with applications, those attacks are noticed best by the user. Following two examples of attacks on this layer.

2.6.1 Malicious code attacks

These attacks include viruses, worms, spyware and Trojan horses. They can attack the operating system and user applications. Often they spread themselves through the network [13].

2.6.2 Repudiation attacks

Identity theft describes this attack. With repudiation attacks an adversary is able to deny an activity he did. So an adversary could login with his account and is able to change session parameters that another user is logged for his activities.

2.7 Multi-layer attacks

Some of the described attacks can perform on different layers (DoS, impersonation attacks, Man-in-the-middle attacks). [13] gives a more specific overview of this type of attacks. Section 2 will now close with the explanation of cryptographic attacks.

2.8 Cryptographic primitive attacks

Attacks in this form use the fact that a random number is only a pseudorandom number and often generated with statistical randomness [13]. Therefore they are not resistant against prediction by cryptanalysts. Another field of these attacks is hash collision, there an adversary tries to find two messages with the same hash value [13].

So far this paper explained different kind of attacks on different layers of the Internet Model. Following different Intrusion Detection Systems are explained whereas main focus lies on the architecture and the algorithms of them.

3 Cooperative Intrusion Detection System

This section describes the first of four, in this paper presented, approaches of IDS. Compared with the three others the cooperative system seems to be classical without special features.

[16] mentioned three important attributes an appropriate IDS should have. First a good system architecture must be found that fits the features of a wireless ad-hoc network. Second suitable audit data sources have to be defined. And last a good model of activities must be found that can separate anomaly when under attack from normalcy.

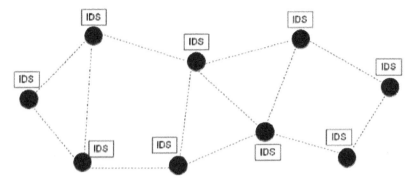

Fig. 2: The IDS Architecture for Wireless Ad-Hoc Network, adapted from [16]

The general architecture of this IDS is shown in figure 2. IDS agents are placed on every node of the network and each agent runs independently and monitors local activities and is able to communicate activities in its communication range. If an intrusion is detected by a local agent the agent initiates response. In the case of anomaly detection in local data or if the evidence is inconclusive and a broader search is warranted, neighbouring IDS agents will cooperate in global intrusion detection actions. All nodes with their IDS agents together form a system wide IDS system of the wireless network [16]. In the next section the parts of an Intrusion Detection Agent are described.

3.1 Intrusion Detection System Agent

An IDS agent is attached on every node of the network. Such agent can be fairly complex [16] but after all it can be split into six main pieces. The next subsection will explain them.

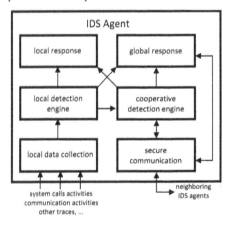

Fig. 3: A Conceptual Model for an IDS Agent, adapted from [16]

7

3.1.1 Local data collection

This module is responsible for gathering streams of real-time audit data from different sources. Those data streams can include system, user and communications activities. A node can include multiple data collection modules [16].

3.1.2 Local detection engine

The local detection engine analyzes local data traces for evidence of anomalies. The IDS agent should use statistical anomaly detection because updating a rule database across an ad-hoc network is not easy. Therefore an anomaly detection model is necessary [16]. This model can be built in following steps:

- Generating of normal profiles

- Generating of deviations from normal profiles

- Computing of detection model from deviation data

In the first step, normal profiles are computed by tracing data from a process where all activities are normal. Then some normal and abnormal activities are recorded. At least the detection model is computed from the deviation data to differ normalcy and anomalies.

3.1.3 Cooperative detection engine

Whenever any node detects an intrusion locally with strong evidence it can independently determine that the network is under attack. If a node detects an intrusion with weak evidence it can initiate a cooperative global intrusion detection procedure. A global intrusion detection is done by propagating the intrusion detection state to all neighbour nodes. An intrusion detection state information can look like this: "With p% confidence, node A concludes from its local data that there is an intrusion" [16].

1. Intrusion state request   - - - →
2. Propagation of state information   - - - - - ►
3. Determination whether majority indicates an intrusion
4. If intrusion is detected to network, node initiates response procedure

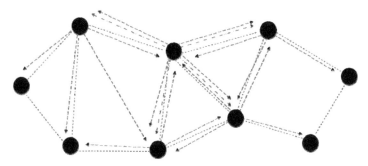

Fig. 4: Global intrusion detection procedure, adapted from [16]

8

After this propagation a distributed algorithm is used to compute a new intrusion detection state for a node, using other nodes information which can include weighted information. The weight of the component could be how far this node is located. Figure 4 shows the message exchange of a global intrusion detection procedure. In the first step the node which initiates the global intrusion detection sends to all neighbouring nodes an intrusion state request. Each node which receives this request (including the initiation node) propagates then the state information which indicates the probability of an intrusion to its neighbours. In step 3 every node determines if the received state report indicates an intrusion or anomaly. If this is the case, then the node concludes that the network is under attack [16]. Every node that detects an intrusion is then able to initiate a response procedure.

It is clear that the audit data of other nodes can not be trusted because it could be compromised and therefore should not be used. Therefore only the intrusion detection state is propagated because a compromised node will not send any report about an intrusion. Hence this scheme of this global intrusion detection works until the majority of nodes are compromised. If this is the case, an intrusion could be detected by strong evidence of a single node [16].

3.1.4 Local and global response

After an intrusion is detected a node initiates a response. There are different possibilities of a response. [16] mentions a re-initialization of communication channels between nodes and an identification of the compromised nodes and a re-organization of the network to preclude the promised nodes. Another possibility is to inform the end-user, who would then initiate appropriate actions. In the next section it is explained how an anomaly can be detected. This important task in ID has to distinguish anomalcy from normalcy.

3.2 Anomaly detection

This section describes how anomaly can be detected in wireless networks. In [16] therefore the ad-hoc routing protocol is chosen to demonstrate the creation of a detection model. The main concern in this example is false routing information which is generated by a compromised node. The requirement of the anomaly detection model is a low false positive rate, calculated as the percentage of normalcy detected as anomalies and a high true positive rate, calculated as the percentage of anomalies detected [16]. Therefore first collecting trace data is necessary which can be used to distinguish between normalcy and anomaly. The routing table consists at the minimum the next hop to each destination node and the distance. A change in the routing table can happen due to physical movement of a node or a change of the membership. For a single node, its own movement and the change in its own routing table are the only reliable information that it can trust [16].

Distance	Direction	Velocity	PCR	PCH
0.01	S	0.1	20	15
10	S	20	80	50
0.02	N	0.1	0	0
...	...	...	...	...

Table 2: Sample Trace Data for Ad-Hoc Routing, adapted from [16]

Therefore data of the node's physical movement and the corresponding change in its routing table is used as the basis of the trace data. Table 2 shows the routing table used in this example, there the movement is measured by distance, direction and velocity. This could be obtained by a GPS device. The changes of the routing table are measured by the percentage of changed routes (PCR) and the positive or negative percentage of changes in the sum of hops of all routes (PCH) [16].

First the diversity of normal situations is simulated for each node. The results of all nodes are then aggregated into a single data set. This data set describes all normal changes in routing tables for all nodes. Following computation scheme is used to compute the normal profile:

1. Denote the class (e.g. PCR) and all features (e.g. distance, direction, velocity, PCH)

2. Split to n classes represent PCR values in n-ranges (e.g. 10 classes, each representing 10 percentage points)

3. Apply a classification algorithm (e.g. RIPPER [1]) to the data and compute classification rules (e.g. "if(distance < 0.01 and PCH < 20) then PCR = 2; elseif ...". Therefore each feature is assigned to a class

4. Go to step 1 and compute classifier for PCH

The computed classification rules for PCH and PCR together describe now normal conditions (= normal profile). During checking an observed data record, the classification rules are applied to the record. Hence a misclassification, e.g. when the rule computes "PCR=3" but in fact it is "PCR=5", is counted as violation [16]. The confidence of the violated rule can be used as deviation score.

PCR deviation	PCH deviation	Class
0.0	0.0	Normal
0.1	0.0	Normal
0.2	0.2	Normal
0.9	0.5	Abnormal
0.3	0.1	Normal
...	...	...

Table 3: Sample Deviation Data, adapted from [16]

If abnormal data is available, there could be deviations shown in table 3. Then the classification algorithm can be applied to compute a classifier. A detection model, which uses this deviation scores, distinguishes then between normal from abnormal. In the case that abnormal data is not available during testing process, normal clusters of the deviation scores can be computed, where each score pair is represented by a point (PCR deviation, PCH deviation).

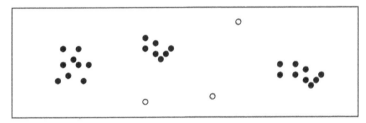

Fig. 5: Cluster build of deviation scores

Outliners who do not belong to a cluster can be considered as anomalies [16]. Figure 5 shows the computation of clusters where black filled dots represents normalcy and white filled dots anomalcy, because they are not a member of a cluster.

In anomaly detection a poor performance, which will be noticeable through a high false positive rate, indicates often insufficient data gathering, insufficient or false chosen features or the usage of a false modelling algorithm. The next section presents a different IDS which tries to act more efficient through the fact that not every node monitors the network traffic.

4 Modular Intrusion Detection System

The architecture presented before in section 3 relies on the fact that every node runs a mobile agent which monitors all traffic of that node and each node is responsible to detect an intrusion. This approach leads to much computation intensive analysis on every node. Also the global intrusion detection procedure is very computation intensive. Because of the limitation in resources this is a huge drawback in ad-hoc networks. Furthermore the network overhead increases due to the propagation of state information. Therefore [5] presents an architecture where a cluster of nodes has only a few mobile intrusion agents. The nodes which run the agent are elected by a distributed algorithm. Those elected nodes are responsible for monitoring the network traffic of the cluster so that the overall network security is not entirely dependent on any particular node. This IDS is built on a mobile agent framework which allows to build different mobile agents [5]. Following the overall architecture is presented.

4.1 Modular Intrusion Detection System architecture

In this approach nodes have different tasks. Possible tasks are:

Network monitoring: only certain nodes have sensor agents for network packet monitoring. This leads to a reduction of needed computational and battery power of mobile hosts.

Host monitoring: every node is monitored internally by a host-monitoring agent. This agent monitors on system and application level.

Decision-making: every node decides on the intrusion threat level on host-basis. Certain nodes collect information and make collective decisions about the overall network-level intrusions.

Action: every node has an action module for resolving intrusions on host-basis e.g. killing a process.

Some classes are present on every mobile node while others are distributed to a selected group of nodes. This approach will minimize power consumption and the IDS related processing time [5].

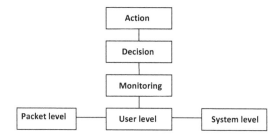

Fig. 6: Layered Mobile Agent Architecture, adapted from [5]

In figure 6 the hierarchy of different agent classes is shown. As mentioned before, some intrusion detection functionality must be efficiently distributed to a small number of nodes of the cluster. These functionalities are the monitoring of network packets and decision making. Every node of the cluster is responsible for host-based monitoring which means the local monitoring of the node. Nevertheless an adequate degree of intrusion detection must be guaranteed [5]. One important task is the selection of network monitoring nodes, how this works is described next.

4.2 Node selection algorithm

First a number must be chosen which stands for the maximum number of hops a decision node is away from any other node. This number affects the network monitoring range, due to only those nodes taking part in a decision process. It is clear that a higher number results in fewer decision nodes. In our example it is set to 1.

The number of neighbouring nodes for node i at cluster setup is denoted as C_i. Every node sends its C_i value to all neighbour nodes.

Every node i receive all C_j values from its neighbours j and sums up the total as S_i which denotes the connectivity index. $S_i = C_i + \sum_j C_j$

The calculated S_i value is then broadcasted with an attached time to live, which equals the number of hops selected in the beginning.

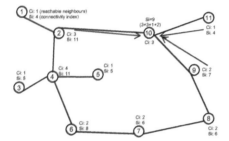

Fig. 7: Computation of connectivity index, adapted from [5]

In figure 7 the process of calculation of the connectivity index is shown. Next to each node the calculated C_i value, which indicates the number of neighbouring nodes and the calculated connectivity index S_i is shown. For node no. 10 the calculation of S_i is emphasized, there it can be seen that every neighbouring node sends first its C_i value to this node. Then it sums up all values to the connectivity index which is in this case 9.

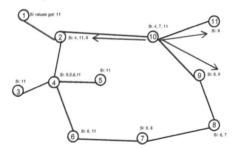

Fig. 8: Broadcasting the Si value, adapted from [5]

The next step, which includes broadcasting the S_i value, is shown in figure 8. Next to each node all S_i values a node got are shown. Node 10 sends therefore its S_i value of 9 to nodes no.

2, 11 and 9. As mentioned before, each node broadcasts its S_i value while the selected number of hops is set as time to live and therefore restricts the broadcast to only neighbouring nodes as the number was set to 1. Now the election can start, therefore every node sends a vote packet to the node which sent the highest connectivity index. In the case that a node receives a vote with the same S_i value as its own, it does not send a vote to the source node. If two nodes have the same S_i value and send simultaneously, the node with the largest total of S_i values sends a *discard vote* to the other. Each node that received at least one vote runs network monitoring and decision agents [5].

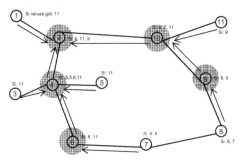

Fig. 9: Election process of network monitoring nodes with max-hop=1

Figure 9 illustrates the sent vote messages of every single node. Emphasized nodes are now elected to act as network monitoring and decision nodes (clusterheads). There now 5 out of 11 nodes are elected. Every node has at least one neighbour which participates in network monitoring. This is due to the selection of the value 1 for the maximum-number-of-hops value. If a node sends a packet, the neighbour of the sending node is responsible to analyze the packet. Figure 9 points out that the entire network is monitored.

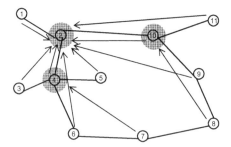

Fig. 10: Election process with max-hop=2

In contrast to figure 9, figure 10 shows the election process when the number of max-hops is set to 2. This means, that every node broadcasts its S_i value to a wider range. Now only 3 out of 11 nodes are responsible for network monitoring and decision making. The saving of the resources will be better, but 3 links are not monitored, because if a node without an elected node sends out a packet, it has no neighbouring node which participates in network

14

monitoring. This would be suitable for highly-dynamic environments because there the network configuration changes often and every link would be monitored at a given time [5].

% of nodes acting as network monitors

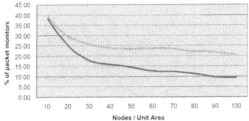

Fig. 11: Percentage of nodes engaged in packet monitoring
in a one-hop (dashed line) and two-hop (solid line) network, adapted from [5]

In figure 11 it can be seen how much nodes will act as network monitoring nodes when a one-hop or two-hop scenario was chosen. Like it was shown before, the two-hop network has less monitoring nodes than the one-hop. Also it comes out that in the case of a smaller network the percentage is higher than in a larger network, while the increase flattens as the network grows. How network monitoring is performed is explained next.

4.3 Network packet monitoring

Each elected clusterhead node monitors only packages sent by a node of its cluster. To avoid double analyzing, only packages where the originator node is a node of the cluster are analyzed. Therefore the same packet is analyzed only once by a network monitoring agent. Packets are inserted in a message queue with a fixed size. If the queue is full, new packets are discarded until the queue has free space. The queue size limits therefore the processing of a node that it can perform regular user tasks [5].

Packet Dropping Rate

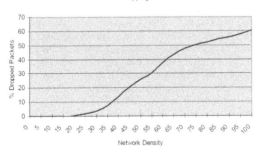

Fig. 12: Increase in packet dropping rate as the network
density increases, adapted from [5]

In figure 12 it can be seen that packet loss, in the case of high network density, can increase up to 60%. Furthermore, each clusterhead node has to perform in decision making, this is described in the next subsection.

4.4 Decision making

Decision making is the second task of each clusterhead. The decision agent contains a state machine for all nodes in the cluster [5]. All occurred intrusions and anomalies are gathered for each node of the cluster by this agents. The agent has also the ability of accessing reports from node's local monitoring agents. So the clusterhead is able to maintain a threat level for every node. When a certain threat level is reached, the clusterhead sends a command to the local agent of the affected node, that an action must be undertaken. Afterwards the clusterhead decreases the threat level in his database [5]. Whereas clusterheads perform in network monitoring and decision making, every node has to do local detection, this task is described next.

4.5 Local detection

Every node of the cluster performs local detection on user and system level. Whenever an anomaly with strong evidence is detected, the local detection agent terminates the suspicious process or re-issues security keys [5]. Of course it is possible to implement other actions in the case of an intrusion. If inconclusive anomaly is detected by the agent, the node is reported to the decision agent of the clusterhead. When more conclusive evidence is gathered about this node from any source, the action is undertaken by the local agent of the node [5].

Following the next IDS is presented. It is very similar to the last one but has some interesting differences.

5 Cluster Based Intrusion Detection System

In [4] a cooperative IDS is presented which has similarities with the system from [5], but tries to fix some problems. It is also a cluster based detection scheme where a monitoring node (clusterhead) is randomly and in a fair way elected. Also the responsibility of intrusion detection is shared among nodes in the cluster. This architecture defines a cluster (CL) as a group of nodes that are close to each other. Close means in this context that the clusterhead has all members in its 1-hop vicinity. Nodes who are not clusterhead are called citizens. In the case that a node cannot be reached by any other node it is defined as a single node cluster (SNC). The size of the whole cluster (clusterhead and citizens) is declared as S_c. Furthermore this architecture attaches much importance to a fair election of the clusterhead. This means every node should have a fair chance to serve as clusterhead. Therefore the election should be fair due to the use of randomness in the election decision process and the clusterhead is periodically re-elected. Besides nodes should not be able to manipulate the selection process to increase or decrease its or another node's chance to be selected. In comparison, other protocols (like [5]) compute a score for every node and the node with maximal score is elected. Thus a node is able to advertise a high score for itself and this do not guarantee a random and fair selection of clusterheads [4]. Following the design of this IDS is explained.

5.1 Possible state of nodes

In this architecture a node can get different states. Initially every node is in the state *INITIAL*. Having this state, every node performs only a local node based intrusion detection. Therefore it acts as single node cluster [4].

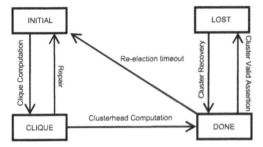

Fig. 13: Finite State Machine of the cluster formation protocols, adapted from [4]

Subsequently the initial clusterhead setup round, including the clique and clusterhead computation, is initiated. Figure 11 illustrates a finite state machine for all possible states of a node. After being in state *INITIAL*, a clique has to be computed, next it is presented how this is done.

5.2 Clique computation

A clique is defined as a group of nodes where every node has a direct link to each other node [4].

Fig. 14: a) Clique before clusterhead computation b) Clique after clusterhead computation

This strict requirement of a clique can be relaxed after a clusterhead is elected. Then only the clusterhead needs a direct link to each member of the cluster. Figure 14a shows the requirement for a clique of 4 nodes before, 14b a possible clique after clusterhead computation. After this computation every nodes of the clique knows all other clique members. After all the nodes enter state *CLIQUE*. Next the clusterhead computation is performed, the next section describes this task.

5.3 Clusterhead Computation Protocol

When the clique is formed and all nodes have the state *CLIQUE*, the clusterhead is computed. Following steps are processed:

- Each node i generates a random number R_i

- Node i broadcasts an *ELECTION_START* message, containing the id of the node and a hash value of the id and R_i *(Id$_i$, Hash(Id$_i$, R$_i$)* attached with a timer T_1.

- When node i received all *ELECTION_START* messages from its clique members, it broadcasts an *ELECTION* message containing *(Id$_i$, R$_i$)*.

- In the case T_1 is timed out, nodes which did not send an *ELECTION* message are excluded from the clique.

- On receiving an *ELECTION* message from node j, node i checks the hash value it got from node j by the *ELECTION_START* message and saves R_i locally.

When all R_i values are received, node i calculates a value $H=SEL^5(R_0....R_{Sc-1})$. All nodes are then ordered and the hth node is elected as clusterhead. The selection function can be any function, [4] mentioned a modular XOR function. This algorithm assures a fair and random selection of nodes.

If node i is now a citizen node, it sends an *ELECTION_DONE* message to the new clusterhead (*H*) and waits until it receives an *ELECTION_REPLY* from *H*. Then it enters *DONE* state.

In the case node i was elected as clusterhead, first it sets a timer T_2. Then it checks if every member of the clique sends an *ELECTION_DONE* message. If T_1 is timeout, every node without an *ELECTION_DONE* message is excluded from the clique. After this, it sends the *ELECTION_REPLY* to all nodes of the cluster and enters also *DONE* state. The next operation which has to be done is the valid assertion which is explained next.

5.4 Cluster Valid Assertion Protocol

Every node in *DONE* state performs periodically an assertion which consists of two parts.

PART ONE

When a link between a citizen C node and the clusterhead H is broken, C checks if it is in another cluster. If C is in another cluster it enters LOST state and activates the *Cluster Recovery Protocol* which is explained later. Moreover H will remove C from its citizen list. If there are no more citizens in the cluster, H becomes also a citizen if it belongs to another cluster. Otherwise H enters *LOST* state and initiates the *Cluster Recovery Protocol* [4].

PART TWO

Also in the case of no change in membershipment, the clusterhead does not perform forever. Because this would be not fair in terms of service and is unsafe in terms of long time-single-point control and monitoring [4]. Therefore there exists a re-election timeout T_r during nodes are in *DONE* state. When T_r expires, all nodes of the clique enter *INITIAL* state and start a new clusterhead setup. If the clique property has not changed, the clique computation can be

---

[5] Selection Function

skipped [4]. Another important protocol is the cluster recovery protocol, which helps nodes if they lost their cluster or clusterheads if they lost all their citizens. The next section describes this protocol.

5.5 Cluster Recovery Protocol

This protocol is initiated whenever a citizen loses its connection to the clusterhead or the clusterhead loses all his citizens. The main task is to re-discover a new clusterhead. Therefore a node i broadcasts an $ADD\_REQUEST$ message, containing ID_i together with a timer T_3. Any clusterhead which receives this request, replies with an ADD_REPLY message containing the id of the clusterhead. Node i replies to the first ADD_REPLY message it received with an ADD_ACK message, containing its id and enters $DONE$ state. Finally the clusterhead adds node i into its citizen list. If T_3 is timed out and no ADD_REPLY message is received there is no clusterhead available. Therefore node i enters INITIAL state and waits for other lost citizens to create a new clique [4]. The last type of an IDS is described in the next section. It differs from the IDS presented before and uses additionally alert aggregation for better results in intrusion detection.

6 Zone Based Intrusion Detection System

A zone based approach [12] with alert aggregation should also lower false positive ratio and higher detection ratio compared to systems with local detection only. The next sections present this approach and introduce alert aggregation. Fist alert aggregation is explained in the next subsection.

6.1 Alert Aggregation

Often isolated events are not considered significant [3]. Thus intrusion detection alerts are aggregated into *situations*. A *situation* is a set of alerts that have certain characteristics in common. An intrusion event contains information that can be used as aggregation axis e.g. Source, Target, Class of attack [3]. Therefore e.g. alerts with same source and target can be aggregated together. In wired networks this approach is often used to give the administrator a better overview of alerts.

IDS Alert					IDS Alarm		
Class	Hostname	Message			Class	Hostname	Message
HARMLESS	WW_Directory	www.org	Suspicious directory cgi-bin		WARNING	A_Situation1	Situation1 (600)	HTTP alerts
HARMLESS	WW_Directory	www.org	Suspicious directory Admin	
HARMLESS	WW_InsecureCgi	www.org	Insecure cgi test-cgi	
HARMLESS	WW_InsecureCgi	www.org	Insecure cgi webadmin.passwd	
HARMLESS	WW_Suspicious Cgi	www.org	Suspicious cgi password	

Fig. 15: IDS Alert and IDS Alarm view, adapted from [3]

The idea behind this scheme is that the administrator has only to look to the alarm window where all security relevant information is displayed in a condensed manner. As example figure 15 shows the aggregation of alerts, where the left window contains every single alert and the right window shows only one alarm, which is generated through aggregation of alerts. If there is the need to view the single alert messages, this is still possible [3]. So this zone based IDS (ZBIDS) also uses alert aggregation to get a better performance. Following the architecture of the Zone Based IDS is presented.

6.2 Zone Based Architecture

In this approach also every node is equipped with an IDS agent. The whole network is divided into nonoverlapping zones, where agents can cooperate [12]. This ZBIDS introduces a two level approach, where at the low-level each IDS agent on every node (intrazone node) monitors locally and reports alerts to the gateway nodes in the same zone. At high-level there are gateway (also called interzone) nodes which have physical connection to other zones' gateway nodes and aggregate locally generated alerts inside its zone. Gateway nodes can utilize alerts to generate alarms which indicate an intrusion. There must be a distinction between alerts and alarms.

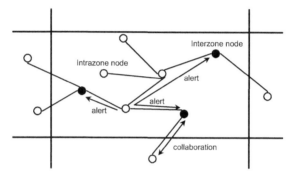

Fig. 16: The Zone-Based IDS, adapted from [12]

Alerts are only generated locally by every intrazone node and reported to gateway nodes whereas an alarm can only be initiated by a gateway node. Moreover gateway nodes from different zones can collaborate to perform ID in a wider area. Figure 16 shows different zones whereby black filled nodes illustrate gateway nodes of the zone in the middle. The advantage of creating zones instead of using a hierarchical architecture is the reduction of costs for generating. A critical point is the selection of the zone size which depends on different factors (node mobility, network density, transmission power, ...). Too large zone sizes can lead to a compromise of the advantage to a hierarchical structure, because broadcasting the alerts involves communication overhead. On the other hand too small chosen zone sizes can lead to problems in aggregation of alerts because of insufficient information. Also this IDS uses agents on nodes, those agents are presented next.

6.3 IDS Agent

The used IDS agent is similar to the one presented in section 3.1 with the exception of

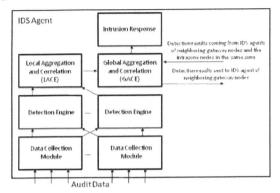

Fig. 17: Diagram of an IDS agent, adapted from [12]

the *Local* and *Global Aggregation and Correlation* (LACE, GACE) module. The LACE module combines detection results of different local detection engines. The task of the GACE module depends on whether it runs on an intrazone or interzone node. If it runs on an intrazone node, it aggregates and correlates the detection rules of intrazone nodes and cooperates with other interzone nodes. In the case GACE runs on an intrazone node, the module transmits all locally generated alerts to the interzone node. All other modules have similar function as mentioned in section 3.1. Collaboration is also essential at this IDS and is presented next.

6.4 Collaboration Mechanism

[12] mentions two possible approaches how interzone nodes can collaborate with their intrazone nodes. The subscription based mechanism allows an IDS agent of an interzone node to subscribe for security related information of an intrazone node. The subscription message contains then only information which is required. It is clear that this approach reduces communication overhead because not every information is sent to the gateway node.

Moreover there exists the local broadcast mechanism. When an agent of an intrazone node generates a local alert, it could propagate the results to its interzone nodes (see figure 16). But when nothing suspicious happened in the last period, there is no need for the local IDS to send security information. Neighbouring gateway nodes can further collaborate with each other through the transmission of the security-related information. This approach avoids global broadcasts. Also it is not necessary to propagate alerts every period inside a zone [12]. These strategies also avoid communication overhead. Last the alert aggregation mechanism is shown, moreover examples of aggregation are presented.

21

6.5 Alert Aggregation Mechanism

Due to wireless ad-hoc network IDS often have high false positive ratio and alert flooding, it is appropriate to use alert aggregation. This should help to reduce false positive alarms and increase detection ratios by aggregating local alerts [12]. Furthermore aggregation also allows better evaluating the progress of an attack [12]. To do so, a data model is needed in form of a class hierarchy to describe alerts.

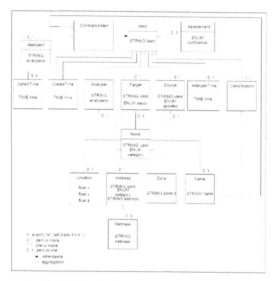

Fig. 18: The alert class hierarchy of ZBIDS, adapted from [12]

[12] introduces a modified version of the *Intrusion Detection Message Exchange Format* (IDMEF) [2] which can be seen in figure 18. IDMEF was proposed by the Intrusion Detection Working Group (IDWG) and aims at wired IDS. In this model different entities are used to describe an alert. Therefore e.g. the classification, target, source or detection time can be used to classify alerts. If a local node detects an anomaly, it generates an alert based on this model. In the approach of [12], gateway nodes make decisions based on the following information from local alerts:

- Classification similarity: Two alerts are aggregated, if their classification fields are the same, which indicates the same occurrence o the attack

- Time similarity: Alerts are aggregated, if the fields DetectTime and CreateTime are the same

- Source similarity: Alerts are aggregated, if the source (IP address of attacker) is the same

So far four different IDS were presented. In the next section a totally different approach is presented by introducing game theory in the context of intrusion detection.

7 Using Game Theory in Intrusion Detection

This last section should show how game theory can influence ID in wireless ad-hoc networks. First this paper gives some basic information of game theory, whereas more specific information is given in [10], [8], [11], [7]. Afterwards ID is formulated as a Bayesian game and an approach is presented how resources can be saved due to a game theoretical scheme.

7.1 Game Theoretical Formulation of Intrusion Detection

Intrusion detection, where an attacker tries to attack an IDS can be seen as a basic signalling game which falls under the category of multi-staged dynamic non-cooperative game with incomplete information [10]. In a signalling game a player A has some private attributes and the opponent B has a belief of them. A is now able to send B a signal whereon B assigns attributes to player A (regarding to his beliefs) and responds in the way that he has the best payoff. Player A anticipates this and chooses his next signal in the way he has the best payoff [11]. Definitions of a signalling game related to ID:

- **Sender**: a node which sends signals

- **Receiver**: a host-based IDS, which receives signal and chooses an action

- **Type**: the attribute of sender (e.g. strong, weak), in the beginning the nature draws the type of sender from a typeset Θ

- **Signal**: the message from the sender

- **Action**: is set by the receiver after receiving a signal

- **Pay-off**: the benefit the player gets at the end of the game/round

- **Belief**: the probability about possible types of the sender, chosen by the receiver

The phrase multi-staged dynamic non-cooperative game with incomplete information means the following:

- **Multi-staged**: the game consists of more rounds, it is no one round game

- **Dynamic**: there is a strict order of play and the players know the history of moves played by others

- **Non-cooperative**: the behaviour of players is self-enforcing, there is no cooperation between players

- **Incomplete Information**: players have some private information (e.g. appetite, strength) and for each a parameter value type

7.2 Bayesian Game Approach for Intrusion Detection

[7] introduce a model for IDS based on a Bayesian game where the intention is to save resources. In the Bayesian context an attacker/defender game can be static or dynamic. A static game does not take the game evolution into account and a defender has fixed beliefs

about the types of the opponent. In a dynamic game, as described in 9.1, a defender can dynamically update his beliefs based on new observations of opponent's actions and the game history [7]. Furthermore, also in this context, this game is an incomplete information game, where the defender is unknown about the types of his opponent. The game is designed as a two player game, where one player is the attacking node and the other the defending node. An attacking node i has a private type [regular/malicious]. The malicious type of i has two strategies [Attack/Not Attack], where the regular type has only one strategy [Not Attack]. Node i also knows the type of the defending node (regular). The defending node j has a public type which is common known [regular] and two strategies [Monitor/Not Monitor]. Node j does not know the type of node i.

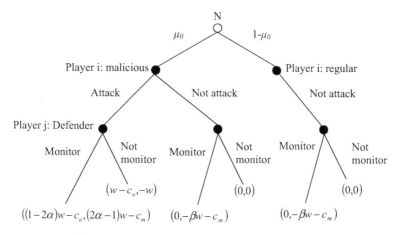

Fig. 19: Extensive form of static Bayesian game, adapted from [7]

At figure 19 the static Bayesian game is shown as a tree. Node N represents the nature node who determines the type of player i the attacker. μ_0 represents the prior probability defender j assigns to player i being malicious.

24

7.2.1 Static game

With a payoff matrix it is possible to calculate the payoff for each player of the game in consideration of the chosen strategy.

	Monitor	Not monitor
Attack	$(1-2\alpha)w-c_a , (2\alpha-1)w-c_m$	$w-c_a , -w$
Not attack	$0, -\beta w-c_m$	$0, 0$

Table 4: Payoff matrix of a malicious player, adapted from [7]

	Monitor	Not monitor
Not attack	$0, -\beta w-c_m$	$0, 0$

Table 5: Payoff matrix of a regular player, adapted from [7]

Tables 5 and 6 show the payoff matrix for a malicious player and a regular player of the attacking node. There α represents the detection or true positive rate of the IDS, β represents the false positive rate of the IDS whereby $\alpha, \beta \in [0,1]$. The costs of attacking and monitoring are denoted as c_a and c_m. The defender's security value is worth w, where $w > 0$. Therefore $-w$ represents a loss of security which value is equivalent to a degree of damage [7].

The payoff matrix for a malicious type of the attacking node is shown in table 5. The matrix can be understood in following way: if the defending node i does not monitor and the malicious player j chooses to attack, then the payoff for i is $-w$ and for j it is $w-c_a$. This is clear because the defending node has a loss which value is the worth of security and the attacking node has w as gain minus the attacking costs c_a. In the case that the malicious node does not attack and the defending node does not monitor, there is no payoff at all. If the defender monitors and the malicious node attacks, then the payoff for the defender is $\alpha w - (1-\alpha)w = (2\alpha-1)w$ which is the true positive rate minus the false negative rate multiplied by the security value ($1-\alpha$ is the false negative rate). On the other side, the gain of the malicious player is the loss of the defender $= (1-\alpha)w - \alpha w = (1-2\alpha)w$ which is the false negative rate minus true positive rate multiplied by the security value. Last if the malicious node does not attack and the defender monitors, the attacker has no gain and the defending node's payoff which is a loss is $-\beta w$ due to false alarms and the costs of monitoring $-c_m$. Table 6 shows the payoff matrix for a regular player of the attacker which only has the strategy [Not Attack] and therefore its equal to the second row of table 5.

It is shown in [7] that no pure strategy BNE exists when $\mu_0 > \dfrac{(1+\beta)w+c_m}{(2\alpha+\beta-1)w}$. Simplified that means if the defender's belief about the maliciousness of the attacking node is high then there exits no pure strategy [7], because a pure strategy exists of only one action. Therefore a mixed strategy is used in that case which means that the defender plays [Monitor] with probability q^* and the attacker plays [Attack] with probability p^* if it is malicious and [Not Attack] if it is of regular type.

A pure strategy exists if $\mu_0 < \dfrac{(1+\beta)w + c_m}{(2\alpha + \beta - 1)w}$ [7]. This means that the defenders belief about the maliciousness of the attacking node is low and therefore a pure strategy exists [7]. This pure strategy is for the defending node [Not Monitor] and for the attacker node if malicious [Attack] and if regular [Not Attack]. Since the probability is low that the attacking node is malicious it is understandable that the pure strategy in this case is not monitor for the defender.

The lessons learned from an IDS approach which relies on a static game is that it is not necessary to monitor all time. Therefore a lot of resources can be saved if the defender has an efficient monitoring strategy implemented which maximizes his expected payoff. The drawback is the fact that it is hard to find a suitable prior probability to start with [7].

7.2.2 Dynamic game

As mentioned a dynamic game can take the games history in consideration. Therefore a defender can update its beliefs about the attacking node according to the evolution of the game. Due to this fact, the mixed strategy depends on the games history. In the first stage of the game there is no history available therefore a prior probability must be chosen. But in subsequent stages the defender is able to update his beliefs based on his observations [7].

Because belief updating requires the defender to constantly observe actions of the opponent at each stage of the game it is impossible to turn the IDS off as suggested at the static approach for IDS. Hence [7] introduce a hybrid approach which consists of lightweight and heavyweight monitoring.

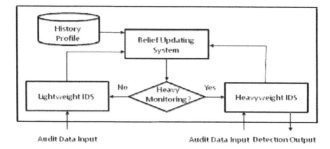

Fig. 20: The Bayesian hybrid detection framework, adapted from [7]

Figure 16 shows this hybrid approach where the decision if heavyweight ID is taken at the next stage depends on the output of the belief-updating-system which uses information from history and the lightweight IDS of the prior round. It must be said that always only one IDS can be running. This approach has the advantage that the system is monitored all time and the defender is able to learn during the game (intrusions) and change his strategy depending on it.

8 Summary

In the sections before this paper introduced four different approaches for ID in wireless ad-hoc networks. A cooperative system (1) in section 3, a modular IDS (2) in section 4, a cluster-based IDS (3) in section 5 and last in section 6 a zone-based IDS (4). All types have in common an intrusion detection agent on every node, whereas the agents in 2,3,4 have different tasks, depending on which node they run. At type 1, every node performs the same tasks for ID and every single node is able to determine that the whole network is under attack. This is one wide difference to the other approaches. That means also that a malicious node could use this fact to affect the whole network. The performance at this architecture is compared to the others also weak, because every node has to perform network and local detection and due to global ID network overhead increases. The approach 2 splits the tasks an agent has to do into network and local monitoring and decision making. In this approach it can happen that the network traffic of some nodes is not monitored which can lead to problems. Also the election algorithm could be improved in the way how the calculation is done. One point e.g. is the fact that every node sums also its own number of neighbours to the connectivity index which is responsible for being elected as network monitoring node. Of course 2 tries to select nodes which can probably perform network monitoring best due to their location.

Attributes	Cooperative IDS (1)	Modular IDS (2)	Cluster Based IDS (3)	Zone Based IDS (4)
IDS agent on every node	yes	yes	yes	yes
Tasks of node's IDS agent	local and network packet monitoring	clusterhead network and local; other nodes local monitoring	clusterhead network and local; other nodes local monitoring	gateway node network and local; other nodes local monitoring
Type of election for monitoring nodes	-	by highest connectivity value	by selection function, result same on every node	-
Re-election	-	in case of network change	periodically	-
Whole network is monitored	yes	depends on value for hop-distance; probably no	yes	yes

Table 6: Comparison of different IDS schemes

Therefore approach 3 builds cliques to give every node same attributes in connection to other nodes. Not till then also a node is elected to act as clusterhead, which is responsible to monitor the network and make decisions about the intrusion state. Moreover the election is done periodically and with the influence of randomness so that every node has the equal service time and the same chance to be elected. Last the zone based approach is more different to 2 and 3. There nodes are separated into zones where also one or more gateway nodes are responsible for network monitoring and intrusion alerting. How alert aggregation really improves ID in the wireless environment could not be determined from [12]. Table 4 lists the most important differences of mentioned IDS schemes.

Furthermore section 7 introduced an approach, how gamy theory can be used to improve ID. Since this paper presents the game theoretical approach more as sidestep, to give a totally different perspective of ID, this approach was not considered in the comparison. Whereas the IDS at the dynamic game approach looks very interesting. There a node monitors either with a heavyweight or a lightweight IDS depending on a history profile. This approach has the advantage that the network is always monitored and it is resource friendly.

9 Conclusions

Intrusion detection in wireless ad hoc networks is due to the lack of infrastructure and the limitation in resources harder to implement than it is in a wired environment. There are a lot of works introducing interesting approaches how to implement ID in ad hoc networks. Most of them have several similarities and differ only in a few facts. For a private end user the task of intrusion detection is mostly unknown in comparison to virus protection. So it is today unthinkable to run a computer without any virus protection software, whereas 10 years ago this was not the normal case. Of course, this results due to the gain of internet access in both, private and business area. Therefore mainly in the field of business, home and private usage, ID seems to be not essential. May in the case of emergency which could occur on battlefields, in hospitals or e.g. in power plants, intrusion detection is another important line of defence. Because there the incentive for an attacker seems to be much higher than disrupting a routing table during a business meeting of five attendees.

Bibliography

[1] W.W. Cohen, *Fast effective rule induction*, in Machine Learning: the 12th International Conference, Lake Taho, CA, 1995

[2] D. Curry, H. Debar, *Intrusion Detection Message Exchange Format Data Model and Extensible Markup Language (XML) Document Type Definition*, Internet Draft, June, 2002

[3] H. Debar, A. Wespi, *Aggregation and Correlation of Intrusion-Detection Alerts*; RAID 2001; Springer Verlag Berlin Heidelberg

[4] Y. Huang, W. Lee, *A Cooperative Intrusion Detection System for Ad Hoc Networks*, Proceedings of the 1st ACM Workshop Security of Ad Hoc and Sensor Netowrks Fairfax, Virginia 2003

[5] O. Kachirski, R. Guaha, *Effective Intrusion Detection Using Multiple Sensors in Wireless Ad Hoc Networks*, in Proceedings of the 36th Hawaii International Conference on System Sciences (HICSS'03)

[6] A. Lintenhofer, *Kryptografische Verfahren und ihre Anwendung*, Studienbrief IT-Security, Version 1.9, Januar 2009, Technikum Wien

[7] Y. Liu, C. Comaniciu, H. Man, *A Bayesian Game Approach for Intrusion Detection in Wireless Ad Hoc Networks*, Valuetools '06, Pisa, Italy

[8] N. Marchang, R. Tripathi; A Game *Theoretical Approach for Efficient Deployment of Intrusion Detection Sytem in Mobile Ad Hoc Networks*; 15th Int. Conference on Advanced Computing and Communications; Guwahati, India

[9] A. Mishra, K. Nadkarni, A. Patcha, *Intrusion Detection in Wireless Ad Hoc Networks*, IEEE Wireless Communications, February 2004

[10] A. Patcha, JM. Park; *A Game Theoretic Formulation for Intrusion Detection in Mobile Ad Hoc Networks*; International Journal of Network Security, 2(2):146-152, March 2006

[11] C. Schäffler, B. Eberwein, D. Lauschke; *Signalisierungsspiele in der Standardform*; Projekt 2006, Ludwig-Masimilians-Universität München

[12] B. Sun, K. Wu, U.W. Pooch; *Alert Aggregation in Mobile Ad Hoc Networks*; WiSE'03 September 19, 2003, San Diego, California, USA

[13] B Wu, J. Chen, M. Cardei, *A Survey of Attacks and Countermeasures in Mobile Ad Hoc Networks*, Wireless/Mobile Network Security, 2006 Springer

[14] H. Yang, H. Luo, F. Ye, S.Lu, L. Zhang, *Security in Mobile Ad Hoc Networks: Challenges and Solutions*, IEEE Wireless Communications, pp. 38-47, 2004.

[15] Y. Zhang, W. Lee, Y.A. Huang, *Intrusion Detection Techniques for Mobile Wireless Networks*, ACM MONET Journal 2002

[16] Y. Zhang, W. Lee, *Intrusion Detection in Wireless Ad-Hoc Networks*, MOBICOM´2000, Boson, Massachusetts

List of Figures

List of Tables

List of Abbreviations

GACE   Global Aggregation and Correlation Engine

ID   Intrusion Detection

IDMEF   Intrusion Detection Message Exchange Format

IDS   Intrusion Detection System

IDWG   Intrusion Detection Working Group

LACE   Local Aggregation and Correlation Engine

ZBIDS   Zone Based Intrusion Detection System